THE INDIAN CAPTIVE

A NARRATIVE

OF THE

Adventures and Sufferings

MATTHEW BRAYTON

IN HIS

Thirty-Four Years of Captivity

AMONG THE

INDIANS OF NORTH-WESTERN AMERICA

Contents

PUBLISHER'S NOTES

The subject of this narrative was a real person. Matthew Brayton, the son of William Brayton, was born in Chicopee, Massachusetts in 1811, which fits with the narrative below. There are long articles about his discovery in several papers, including the *Ohio Repository* newspaper (Canton, Ohio) dated December 6, 1859 and the *Berlin City Courant* (Berlin, Wisconsin) dated November 15, 1860. In both of those papers, his father's name is given as Elijah.

ORIGINAL PREFACE

The following brief narrative of the unparalleled adventures of Matthew Brayton is compiled for the satisfaction of those who wished to preserve a memorial of his romantic history.

Extraordinary as the incidents may appear, there is abundant proof of their entire truth. Living witnesses bear testimony to the circumstances of the mysterious loss of the hero, and his identity is established by incontrovertible proofs. Numerous circumstances also confirm the account given by him of his adventures during the thirty-four years spent among the Indians.

THE LOST CHILD

That portion of North-western Ohio, situated to the South-east of the Black Swamp, was but sparsely settled at the-close of the first quarter of the present century. The hardy pioneers who had left their New England homes to open up the Western wilds, here and there built their modest dwellings and tilled the few acres won from the dense forest and luxuriant prairie. The dusky aborigines, driven from all other parts of Ohio, clung tenaciously to this comparatively neglected spot, and the smoke from the log hut of the settler rose within sight of the Indian wigwam. The two races were at peace with each other, for neither cared to convert a passive neighbor into an active enemy. The Indians had realized their inability to drive back the constantly advancing wave of civilization, and the white settlers had no desire to provoke the savage retaliations of their dusky neighbors unless compelled by necessity to do so.

In the neighborhood of the junction between the Sandusky and Tymochte rivers, in Wyandot county, a remnant of the once powerful Wyandot tribe still remained. One of their villages was at Upper Sandusky, and another at Springville, in Seneca county. A small band of Senecas were also located in the neighborhood, and some scattered Ottawas had their wigwams on Blanchard's Fork, a few miles to the west of the Wyandot settlements. An Indian trail led from Upper Sandusky to Springville, and thence, through the Black Swamp, to Perrysburg. At the latter place it crossed the Maumee, and reached the shore of the Detroit river opposite Malden, in Canada. Some of the Indians living in the North-west of Ohio had sided with the British in the war of 1812, and these annually crossed over to Malden to receive their presents of guns, ammunition and blankets. The Canadian Indians sometimes visited their dusky brethren in Ohio, and thus the trail was frequently traversed.

Among the settlers who had located themselves in the neighborhood of the Wyandot villages was Elijah Brayton, a thrifty farmer from New England, who had established himself near the Tymochte river in what is now Crawford township, Wyandot county. In the year 1825, Mr. Brayton was thirty-nine years of age, and his family consisted of his wife and their six children, William, Harriet,

Lucy, Matthew, Mary and Peter. In that year Mr. Brayton was busy erecting a mill on the Tymochte, and towards the fall of the year he went to Chillicothe for the purpose of bringing up the mill-stones. The journey at that time was long and tedious, and the home affairs were entrusted in his absence to Mrs. Brayton and the eldest son William, then a lad of sixteen.,

On, the 20th of September, 1825, William Brayton, with his younger brother Matthew, then nearly seven and a half years old, started out to hunt up some stray cattle. They proceeded for two or three miles in the direction of the spot where William Brayton at present lives, but found no traces of the missing cattle. Here they met a neighbor named Hart, who was also looking for stray cattle. Matthew had become tired, and declared his inability to proceed any farther. After a short consultation it was agreed that William Brayton and Hart should proceed in search of the cattle, and that Matthew should take the path which led to the house of Mr. Baker, about sixty rods distant, where he could amuse himself with his young playmates until the return of William. The two set out on their cattle hunting expedition, leaving little Matthew to pursue his way along the narrow and ill-defined path.

At the close of the day's search, William Brayton called at Mr. Baker's house for his little brother. To his astonishment he learned that Matthew had not been seen by any of the family. He then turned his steps homeward, thinking that Matthew had changed his mind and gone home, but on arriving there no tidings of the missing boy met him. The alarm and apprehension that filled the breast of the mother may be conceived. A thousand fearful thoughts flitted through her mind in rapid succession. But no time was lost in useless grieving. The men and women who braved the dangers of frontier life were quick to think and prompt to act. A little party turned out at once to search for the missing boy and restore him, if possible, to the anxious household. From the spot where the brothers had parted, the path to Mr. Baker's house was narrowly searched, and the marks of the child's feet were clearly discernible. At no great distance from the commencement of the path it was intersected by a track made by some logs recently drawn from the

4

woods. At this point the traces showed that Matthew had stopped in doubt. They also showed that he had finally taken the log track in mistake for the regular path. Up that track his little footsteps were traced for some distance, but, after awhile, they became fainter, and at last disappeared altogether. The woods on the margin of the track were searched in vain for traces of his feet.

The Indian trail, before spoken of, crossed the log track near where the footsteps became invisible, and it was possible that he had taken that trail; but his footmarks—if he had really followed that path—had been obliterated by the feet of passing Indians.

The party sorrowfully returned from their unsuccessful search, and met the anxious mother with heavy hearts. The night that followed was one of sleepless agony to Mrs. Brayton. To what suffering, or dreadful fate her little boy might be subjected, it was impossible to conjecture, but the dark night and the lonely woods were fraught with dangers to him and with terror to her. The absence of the father at this critical juncture on so long and distant a journey, aggravated the troubles and distress of the time.

Morning broke at last, and never was daylight more eagerly welcomed. With the first dawn of light, messengers set out in all directions for assistance, and soon the woods were astir with searching parties. The Indian villages were examined, but the Wyandots professed entire ignorance as to the movements of the missing boy, and joined with much zeal in the search. The relations between the Braytons and the Wyandots had been of the most friendly character, and there seemed to be no possible reason for their interfering with the peace of that family. They stated, however, that a party of Canadian Indians had passed up the trail on the day that the boy disappeared, but could not say whether he had been carried off by that party or not. Another night came, and again the sorrowful mother met the dejected hunters at her door and received no consolation. At daybreak the parties again set out to search new tracts of country, but all without avail. Mr. Bowe, still remembered in the neighborhood, acted as store keeper of the party, and filled the bags of the searchers with meal as they returned from their long expeditions. The settlers for many miles around turned out in the exciting hunt. Days lengthened into weeks, and* then it became evident that all farther search was useless. Every foot of territory for miles around had been examined and no trace of the lost child could be discovered. He could scarcely have wandered off and perished by starvation or wild beasts, for in either case some trace would have been left. The only inference remaining was that he had been snatched up by the party of Canadian Indians and carried off into hopeless slavery, if not to meet a horrible death. Pursuit now was useless, had the boy been thus carried off, and the search was reluctantly abandoned.

Meantime Mr. Brayton had returned from his journey, and the sad affliction that had befallen his house, fell with crushing weight on his heart. For the sake of his wife and remaining children he bore up nobly, but his distress was keen, and every straw of hope that floated by was eagerly clutched at. From time to time came vague rumors of the boy having been seen in different directions, and the faintest hope of success sufficed to send off the bereaved father or some trusty messenger to follow up the clue, but always without success. The last information that assumed the appearance of probability was received in 1829, from a man who had been traveling among the Indian tribes of Illinois, and who asserted that he had seen among the Indians of that country a white child whose age and appearance corresponded generally with that of the missing Matthew Brayton. Without an hour's delay Mr. Brayton wrote to General Cass, then Indian Commissioner, but his answer crushed out the last remnant of hope. The letter bade the anxious father to renounce all hope based on such a rumor, for there was no such white child among the Indians of Illinois. On what authority the General based his assertion, cannot be said, but it is more than probable that in this he was mistaken.

The weary years passed on but brought no comfort to the stricken household. As all strong impressions fade in the course of time, so faded away the memory of the loss from the minds of men. But deep in the hearts of the parents remained the image of the lost boy, and the thrilling scenes and emotions connected with the search of him recurred again and again long after others had nearly forgotten the incidents. The father never forgot him. His "lost Matthew" was ever in his heart, and his name was often on his tongue. The oldest brother, William, could not forget him, for the mother's reproaches, silent or spoken, for his neglect in sending so young a boy alone on such a path, sank deep into his heart. And could the mother that bore him forget the missing lamb of the fold? The paling cheek, the wasting form, the decaying strength told how deep the love, how bitter the anguish of the mother for her lost son. If she were but sure of his fate—if but one rag of his clothes, but a particle of his body, had remained to assure her that her darling had perished by wild beasts, or been slain by still wilder men, it would at least have given rest to her weary heart; but this torturing mystery was too great to be borne. So the years dragged slowly onward, and each succeeding anniversary of her boy's loss drove the sharp grief still deeper into her heart, until sixteen years after the loss, she tired of this world, and the peaceful turf closed over her sorrows. In her last thoughts the memory of the lost boy had a place. She died of a broken heart.

Matthew Brayton was born April 7th, 1818, and was therefore seven years, five months and thirteen days old at the time of his loss.

MATTHEW BRAYTON'S NARRATIVE

The first seven or eight years of my captivity among the Indians were so full of changes that I cannot distinctly remember the events that occurred, and I am compelled to trust to the accounts given me by the members of the various tribes who were cognizant of the circumstances. From their statements I learn that I was taken from Ohio by a party of Canadian Indians, and by them borne to their village in Canada. The only motive alleged to me for the theft was that the party who stole me had a difference with some white families in Ohio, and that l was taken out of revenge. Among these Indians I remained secreted for some time, the tribe fearing to let me be seen by white men lest I should be taken away.

From all that I can learn, I remained some six or seven months with this tribe, and was then sold to a party of Pottawottomies, who took me across to Michigan. The compensation obtained for me by the Canadian tribe consisted of three and a half gallons of whiskey. With my new owners I remained about half a year, when the Pottawottomies either being afraid to keep me any longer, or having an unappeasable thirst for whiskey, traded me off to the Paw-Paws for five and a half gallons of firewater. I could not say how long I remained in Michigan with this tribe, but I was at length transferred to the Winnebagoes of Illinois, my value having increased with my age to the amount of seven and a half gallons of whiskey. I did not remain long with this tribe, but was sold to the Wisconsin Chippewas for nine and a half gallons of whiskey, and with them remained one year. From the Chippewas I passed into the hands of the Siouxs in Minnesota, and remained with them nearly three years. During my stay with the Siouxs I visited the site of what now forms the city of St. Paul. In that vicinity there were then seven shanties or huts, made of poles and sticks set up endways. Two or three French and Dutch,' with some Indians then occupied the place.

About the ninth year of my captivity among the Indians, the band of Siouxs to which I belonged made an expedition westward. In the course of their hunt they came on a tribe of Snake Indians. The Snakes and Siouxs were generally at war, but there was peace between these two parties. Some differences that had occurred between the bands were settled at the meeting, and the Siouxs celebrated the fact by a great Dog-Dance.

This dance is peculiar to the Siouxs, and I never saw it at any other time. The manner of doing it was this:—A party of warriors squat around in a circle, smoking and talking. A dog is then taken and its legs tied, after which it is thrown into the circle of warriors. One of the "medicine men" kills the animal with his tomahawk, cuts open its side and takes out its liver, which is cut into strips and hung on a pole nearly the height of a man. The warriors spring to their feet and commence dancing around it; all the while smacking their lips and making grimaces as if they were anxious to have a taste of the delicious meat. In a short time one of the dancers makes a grab at the liver and bites off a piece, which he chews and swallows as he dances. Then the others follow his example until all the liver is eaten. If any of the pieces should drop, the "medicine man" picks it up and carries it in the palm of his hand for the dancers to eat, after doing which they lick his hand. As soon as the liver is all eaten, the warriors sit down as before, and wait to see if another dog is thrown in. As long as any one gives a dog, they are compelled to eat its liver raw and warm, and no one is allowed to handle it except the "medicine man." Women are forbidden to join in this dance. The Siouxs think that those who thus eat the liver of the dog will possess that animal's bravery and sagacity.

Before the meeting was over, the Snakes took a great fancy to me, and in order to celebrate their new made truce the Siouxs offered to trade me to the Snakes for eleven gallons of whiskey, which was done, and I was once more transferred to new masters.

My new owners made me change my dress and paint to conform to their style, and I was adopted into the tribe. An Indian who had lost a son in battle took me into his family, and from that time forth I was told to consider him as my father, and his squaw as my mother. But although thus made one of themselves, the Indians did not fail to treat me with considerable harshness, and I was compelled to do some of the severe drudgery usually imposed on the women.

The Snakes at that time hunted in Iowa, but in about a year after my joining them they had repeated quarrels with other tribes, and with the whites. For a few months they remained in Missouri, but eventually packed up and struck the trail for the west side of the Rocky Mountains. Our tribe hunted through Utah for a while, but quarreled with the tribes already in that country, and therefore we once more pushed west, and crossing the mountains that divided us from California, entered that country. Here we lived, for about five years, generally in peace, but having occasional skirmishes with the Digger Indians.

These Indians are a wretched and degenerate race, cowardly, treacherous, filthy and indolent. Instead of living by hunting, as was the case with our tribe, and nearly all the others east of the California Mountains, these obtained a scanty subsistence by digging for roots. The women do the digging whilst the men stay in the lodges or are playing at some game. I have seen hundreds of the women at a time out in this employment. They carry on their backs heavy baskets of the shape of old fashioned straw beehives, and in their hands long sticks with which to dig the roots. Early in the morning they go out and keep at work until evening, when they return with their baskets full of roots. Sometimes they procure enough not only for their present eating, but to lay up for winter use.

The men among the Digger Indians wear very long hair, but that of the women is cut short. Both are nearly naked, and filthy in the extreme. Most of them are tatooed, the women especially displaying in general a large number of designs on their person. They do this merely for ornament, and not for the purpose of showing a difference in rank as is the case in most tribes where the custom exists.

Their houses or lodges are very simple. In the summer they put a number of bushes together in the shape of a cone, and into this they creep for shelter from the sun by day, and to sleep by night. These lodges or tents are more designed to keep off the rays of the sun than for shelter from inclement weather. For the cold and wet seasons the Diggers in the northern part of California have a different kind of dwelling. They dig a pit several feet deep, of the size of the proposed lodge. Then they drive poles into the earth around the edge of the pit, and bend them over so that they will meet at the top, where they are fastened together, making a covering over the pit. They then cover the whole building with earth to the thickness of several inches, or even a foot, leaving a small hole at the top to serve as a chimney., Another hole is made at the side, large enough to admit the body. When they wish to sleep they build a fire in the center of the lodge, then creep in feet foremost and lie in that position to the fire.

The Diggers have a curious way of marrying. When a man takes a fancy to a girl and wants her as his squaw, he speakes to her parents and talks to her a little. Then he lies down with her, and if she lies still they are considered man and wife; but if she gets up and runs away, the courtship is at an end, and the man never tries to get her again. A Digger man can have as many wives as he chooses, but the woman can only have one husband.

When a Digger dies they bum him, with all his implements, and have a great mourning during the ceremony. They believe that when a man dies his spirit goes to the East, and keeps going until it comes to a great water. A large boat is there to take him over. All the good get safely across and go to a very large house where they eat, drink, and gamble, until they are tired* when they go off among the trees. The bad people who go in the boat reach the middle of the water, when the bottom falls out, and they are lost forever.

Whilst in California we frequently visited what is now San Francisco, but which was then a small village of a dozen houses, known by the Spaniards as "Yerba Buena." A few French and Spanish traders were the only white residents, and to those we carried down bear meat, buffalo robes, and furs of various kinds, together with small bits of gold found in the mountains, receiving in exchange blankets and "snakyeye," or whiskey. These trips were made several times during the year, but were finally terminated by the occurrence that resulted in our leaving that part of the country. A large party of Diggers surprised a small hunting party of Snakes and took from them their ponies. A number of warriors were sent out from our tribe to demand them back, but the Diggers had surrendered the ponies to the Spaniards, and now asked their protection from the vengeance of the Snakes. The Spaniards granted their request, and warned our party off. As soon as the news arrived at the Snake village, there was a general excitement, and all who were able to bear arms at once took the war path. The Diggers fled, but were tracked to the coast, where they were supported by several Spaniards. We attacked their camp at daybreak, and a desperate fight ensued. The Diggers are generally lazy and cowardly, but their numbers far exceeded ours, and they were assisted by white men. In the end we were victors, and our party mercilessly tomahawked and scalped all within their reach. Nearly a hundred and fifty scalps were borne off in triumph by the Snakes, and among the trophies were the scalps of some white men.

The result of this fight was a general movement of the whites on the one hand and the California tribes on the other, to drive us out of the country. For a time our tribe stood its ground, but at length it became evident that we could not remain peaceably in that region, so we once more turned our faces eastward and re-crossed the mountains to Utah.

During our stay in this Territory, which did not exceed six or seven moons, our principal encampment was on the banks of the Great Salt Lake, near the present site of Salt Lake City. At that time not a white man lived in that vast wilderness, though not many years afterwards a large city sprang up where our wigwams had formerly stood.

Once more our tribe became restless and dissatisfied with their location, and we changed our hunting ground to Oregon, remaining there about two years. Here we came into collision with the Blackfeet Indians, one of the most ferocious and cruel tribes in existence. They are always at war with the tribes around them and make long journeys for the purpose of attacking some other nation. Several skirmishes took place between our bands and those of the Blackfeet, in which sometimes one and sometimes the other would be successful. In order to defend ourselves from the attacks of the Blackfeet, our tribe made an alliance with the Flat Heads. These are a very singular race who strap boards on the heads of their children so as to change their shape. There are two kinds of Flat Heads, those who have the head flattened from the forehead back, making the head look like a wedge with the sharp edge in front, whilst the others have the sides flattened so as to have the point of the wedge upwards. The party allied with us were of the former kind. A part of the Utahs also joined us about this time, as did the Crees.

Our associated tribes kept going farther north, not finding any place to settle owing to the constant attacks of the Indians through whose territories we passed. With the Bloods and the Blackfeet we had repeated fights until we got above their country, beyond the territory of the United States and into the country of the Copper Head Indians, who roamed over a vast extent of territory extending to the Esquimaux on the North.

Our associated tribes united in the North with the Copper Heads, and here the whole lived in undisputed possession from that time to the present.

NARRATIVE CONTINUED

The Snakes and Copper Heads are ruled over by one General Chief, or Inkupudia,* who remains in power for life unless deposed by the vote of all the tribes. Since the union of the tribes there has been but one General Chief, now (in 1860) eighty years of age, named O-wash-kah-ke-naw. He reigns supreme to a certain extent and appoints sub-chiefs to govern the different tribes. These sub-chiefs are appointed for a period of time and not for life. The General Chief makes known his laws or decrees for the government of the tribes in various matters, and if is the duty of the sub-chiefs to communicate these decrees to the tribes under their charge. The laws in relation to stealing are very strict. Any one proved to have stolen from a person belonging to the associated tribes is condemned to death, ana is generally burned at the stake. It is looked upon as very disgraceful for an Indian to tell a lie to his fellows.

*Not to be confused with Inkpaduta, the Sioux chief of the Spirit Lake Massacre.—Ed. 2015

The men dress with leggins fastened to their moccasins. The leggins extend up to the knees. A tunic of furs is worn about the waist, and the bare place between the tunic and the leggins is daubed with oil and paint. From the waist upwards the body is daubed with oil and paint, and the hair is worn long, extending down over the breast and back. The women are dressed in a somewhat similar manner.

The men do nothing but hunt and fight, leaving the women and captives to do the drudgery. The women are very hard worked, having to collect wood for fires, cut up the game, carry the heavy burdens and do the other work which the warrior considers beneath his dignity to perform.

They are very hardy and can perform with ease labors which many white men would shrink from.

The marriage laws vary among different tribes. Among the Copper Heads the marriage is for life. The Utahs marry for twelve moons, and if at the end of that time they separate they cannot re-marry at any subsequent time. If there is a boy born of the marriage, it goes with the father, and if a girl the mother takes it. The Snakes marry for three years, and if after that time they choose to live together they are married for life.

The birth of a child is accomplished without any trouble or assistance from either doctor, midwife or nurse. The mother retires to her lodge, or if on the march, steps aside and spreads her blanket, and in the course of two or three hours she is up and about her accustomed work, or on the march, as if nothing had happened.

The child, when young, is wrapped around with bandages, strapped to a board and carried on the mother's back. When in the lodge, or at any other time that she wishes to take the child down, the board with the infant on it is set to lean against the wall or is hung to a peg.

As soon as a boy is able to run about his education for the chase and the war path is commenced. A bow three and a half feet long, strung with the sinews of the deer or elk, is placed in his hand, and a bundle of two feet arrows, with flint heads and feathered shafts, is given him. With these he practices at a mark until he is proficient. A board is then set up and a circle about six inches in diameter is described on it. The young Indian takes his position at a short distance from the board and commences throwing his knife at it with the endeavor to strike the center of the circle. When he succeeds in doing this frequently, he increases his distance from the board, and keeps on retreating until he can strike the circle with unerring aim from as great a distance as his strength will permit.

The tomahawk practice comes next. A mark is described on the bark of a tree, and the young Indian throws his tomahawk at it with great force, endeavoring to make it whirl three times in the air, and then to strike with the sharp pick at the back of the axe head so that it shall remain sticking in the mark. As in the knife practice, success at one distance is immediately followed by a retreat of a few paces until the feat can be accomplished at a considerable distance. The same routine is gone through with the axe part so that it shall cleave the bark in the very center of the mark. At about ten years of age, a long bow with arrows of proportionate length, is put into the hands of the boy, and when he becomes of sufficient age to manage it properly he is instructed in the use of the rifle.

The boys are incited to begin hunting and trapping early, and their first success in trapping a beaver, shooting a martin or spearing a muskrat is celebrated with as much triumph as is the first scalp taken in battle by a young-warrior. When about twelve years old the boys join the hunting parties, and are very expert in the use of the bow. Many widows are supported entirely* by their sons who have just passed their twelfth year.

The small children and the very old people are allowed the use of cooked meat, but all others eat their food raw. No salt is used but pepper is frequently obtained from the Russian and Hudson Bay trading posts, and is eaten with the food as a great addition. Besides the privilege of eating cooked meat the very old people are well cared for by the tribe, and are allowed to remain in their lodges without being called out to hunt or work. Everything is done for them and they enjoy perfect rest until their death.

The Copper Heads do not, in general, bury their dead in the same manner with many of the tribes in the United States territory. In some cases, when a warrior dies, the dead body is placed in a birch bark canoe in which are also laid the dead warrior's rifle, tomahawk, pipe, knife and all the other articles belonging to him when alive. Two blankets and provisions to last six months are also placed in the canoe. A poor miserable dog is next procured and hung up by the hind legs to a tree or pole stuck in the ground. The throat of the dog is cut and the animal suffered to bleed to death. The object of this ceremony is to provide a dog to hunt with in the spirit land and the bad blood is let out so as to fit the animal for its new sphere of existence. A poor dog is as serviceable as a good one for the happy hunting grounds if the bad blood is taken out. Some powdered roots are then sprinkled over the body, and the canoe with its contents is launched on the river, if there is one in the neighborhood, and the deceased warrior goes on his way to the happy hunting grounds. If there is no river near, the canoe with its contents is placed on the branches of a tree, or on a temporary scaffold, and left there.

Sometimes in conformity with the wishes of the deceased the body is buried under the roots of a tree or placed in a hollow log to wait until there is some good company to join in the journey to the happy hunting grounds.

The religion of these tribes is very simple. They worship the Great Spirit by standing and praying with arms uplifted to the sky. At times when they see a dark storm-cloud rising up the sky they address it, believing the Great Spirit to be hid within it. After a prayer, on some particular occasions, they drink "snakyeye" or whiskey, and dance with whooping and yelling. They do not believe in a place of punishment hereafter. Those who have committed crimes in this world will be punished here by their tribe, or else the Great Spirit will visit them with sickness or trouble. After this life is over, the spirits all go to the happy hunting grounds, where there is plenty of game and where no enemies will come to disturb them.

MAKING PIPES

The territory occupied by the Copper Heads and the associated tribes lies west or the Rocky Mountains in the high latitudes, extending so far north as the Russian possessions. Their hunting grounds cover a space of several hundred miles, and the natural characteristics of the country are much diversified. Barren mountain ranges alternate with wide plains, fruitful valleys and dense forests. We met with but few rivers in our hunt, but from the Esquimaux and a few stragglers belonging to tribes on the east side of the mountains we had reports of many rivers and big waters on the other side. Our northern head-quarters was about three weeks' journey from the Artie ocean. To the northeast of us, about two weeks' journey, was Big Esquimaux village.

The climate in the northern part of our hunting grounds is cold through the greater part of the year and the ground mostly covered with snow. The trees in this region are of pine, cedar, white hemlock and some other kinds. During the greater part of the year they remain bare, but as soon as the temperature begins to moderate a little the leaves come out about the size of a squirrel's ear. They continue out but for a short time, when they drop off, and the tree is once more bare. The elk, reindeer and the ponies of the Indians all feed on the bark of the trees and the moss.

Snow falls repeatedly during the year, but no rain. There are numerous storms.

With the Esquimaux, who live on the shores of the Arctic Ocean, our tribes often had skirmishes. The Esquimaux are a dirty people, generally short, thick set, with matted hair, and afflicted with the scurvy. They wrap themselves up in furs and live on any kind of carrion. They will eat worms, bugs or snakes when they cannot get game; but their-principal luxury is oil. They make oil from the carcasses of the animals they obtain and enjoy it as a great luxury. They live in huts made of snow and ice, and when moving from place to place they have tents made of furs and skins. In traveling, they use sleds drawn by reindeer and dogs. The Copper Heads never have sleds, but use ponies and elk, both for riding and packing game and other burdens.

The Copper Heads principally traded with the Russian posts, and made trips to them several times a year. They also sent an expedition twice a year to the Red River settlement, and from there to St. Paul. All the dried meats, furs and other articles are packed on the backs of ponies and elks or carried by women and such captives as are in the keeping of the tribe. The mode of packing on the backs of women is for a belt, three fingers wide, to be passed across the forehead and lie down the back. The pack is placed so as to rest on the bottom of the belt and lie on the shoulders, and neck. The bearer is obliged to stoop forward in walking, and the back is frequently bent from this cause. Being a captive, I was sometimes compelled to carry a load but about fifteen pounds less than my own weight, and the squaws have to carry within about twenty pounds of their own weight.

From the Russians we obtained blankets, powder, rifles and other necessary articles in exchange for furs and dried meats. Among other things purchased of the Russians the tribe possessed a compass and a watch, enclosed in a copper case. They learned the use of the compass sufficiently to enable them to travel by its aid.

The lodges are made of poles stuck in the ground and tied together at the top so as to leave a hole in the center. Furs and skins are then fastened around and made tight, except at the entrance. A fire is built in the center of the lodge and the members of the lodge creep in and sleep with their feet to the fire and their heads to the side of the lodge.

In traveling, when the snow is on the ground and the party do not take the lodge fixtures along, the snow is stamped down and blanket spread on the hardened snow. On this the Indian lies down and rolls himself up in the blanket. With this mode of sleeping there is no danger of taking cold.

When the snow is very deep and light the hunters wear wide snow shoes to prevent their sinking at every step. The ponies are also shod with wide moccasins stuffed with hair when the snow is so deep that they cannot travel with ease.

The beasts of burden used by the Indians are ponies, elks and dogs. Both elks and ponies have to be broken into submission to man before they can be used. When the Indians want to break in a pony for riding, one of them mounts a well broke pony, and, after riding around for a little while, suddenly dashes up to the untamed pony, and seizing it by the mane, leaps on its back. The first effort of the surprised animal is to throw the unexpected burden over its head, or failing in this to rise on its hind legs and throw its rider backwards. To prevent either of these purposes being accomplished the rider clasps his arms around the neck of the pony and crosses his legs under its belly so that the toes are inserted between the forelegs of the animal. By these means the pony is rendered unable to jerk the rider off in any direction. Foiled in its efforts to dislodge the unusual encumbrance on its back the pony generally sets off in a wild gallop, in which it is indulged by the rider, and an unexpected difficulty of breathing soon brings the unruly beast to terms. As soon as it gets somewhat tired of its useless excitements, the rider steals his hand down to its nose and there holds some sugar and salt. If the animal prove insensible to the temptation thus held out, the rider gradually works his hand up until he gets some of the mixture into its mouth. The taste of these articles is generally sufficient to subdue the strong will of the pony, and to complete the work the rider puffs tobacco smoke up its nostrils. It is now thoroughly broken in, and will sit easily under a rider or follow its owner like a dog. The Indian never abuses his horse, but always treats it as a friend.

The elk is of great service to the Indians in high latitudes, and shares with the pony the attentions of its owner. The method of catching and taming elk is for one hunter to throw a lasso, or running noose at the end of a long line, on one horn, whilst another hunter does the same to the other horn. The lines are then quickly made fast to two trees, and the hind legs tied to two other trees in a similar manner. Whilst thus fastened in a nearly immovable position the man who is to break in the animal comes up and leaps on his back. The ropes are simultaneously cut by the other Indians, and the elk dashes off with its burden. The rider embraces the horns with his arms and crosses his feet below the belly of the animal, as in breaking ponies. The elk pursues his headlong career for miles, the branching horns preventing his dashing among the trees in such a manner as to hurt the rider. After the elk is thoroughly spent by his long scamper, it is treated in the same manner as in the case of ponies.

The weapons of the Snakes and Copper-Heads consist of rifles, bows and arrows, spears, tomahawks, hunting knives, scalping knives, and war clubs. The arrow heads are made of flint, and much care is used in digging up, selecting and splitting the proper kind of flint. The pipes are also made of flint, and take a large amount of patience and labor in their manufacture. The pipe I made for my self was first squared out from a flint and then drilled with a steel implement, worked by hand. I worked thirty days to complete the boring process, using bear's oil and water to moisten the stone. After the hole was bored, another steel chisel was taken, and the pipe chipped into proper shape. In doing the chiseling, the pipe was placed between two other stones to act as a vice, and the whole pressed between my knees. Then I chipped away, using my clenched hand as a mallet. After the pipe and been chipped into shape and then ornamented with cut designs, it was first oiled and then dyed a pale red with a pigment extracted from a root. A stem of cherry or other wood inserted in this pipe completes it.

THE ATTACK

Hunting is the principal occupation of the Indians, and their only means of subsistence. The climate does not admit the raising of crops, even if the Indians were disposed to till the ground, which they are not. During the fall the camps are removed to the lower part of the British territory in order to hunt the buffalo.

To show how the buffalo are killed, I will relate my experience on one of the hunts in which I was engaged.

Our hunting party, with the families of the hunters, traveled for seven days before reaching the traces of any herds. A few stray bulls were killed, and some of their flesh eaten, but it was too hard and tough for good eating. At length we arrived at the place where there were strong hopes of finding buffalo, and our camp was fixed. Early next morning the hunting party rode off, leaving the squaws and children to make arrangements for preparing the meat when it should be brought to the camp.

After riding a short distance, we came on traces of a large herd, and then rode forward in high spirits. We soon came in sight of some bulls feeding quietly, and beyond them could discover a large herd of cows. The difference between the sexes can be seen at a long distance by their mode of herding. The bulls feed singly, and are scattered over the prairies, whilst the cows huddle together as if for protection. The bulls are the most savage, but the cows are the fleetest of foot, and are very difficult to approach. Their flesh is, however, more highly esteemed than that of the bulls, it being more tender and juicy.

On reconnoitering the respective groups it became evident that we could not reach the cows without first breaking through the herd of bulls, and this we prepared to do at once. Riding slowly up so as not to alarm them, we approached within a few hundred yards of them before they took much notice of us. Then they ceased feeding and commenced bellowing furiously.

At this the signal was given, and our fleet ponies were spurred rapidly towards the herd. When close to them, each hunter singled out a buffalo, and dashing impetuously past the animal, discharged an arrow into its neck. Those whose arrows did not fatally wound the beasts were at once exposed to imminent danger, as nothing exceeds a wounded buffalo in ferocity and strength. Rising for a moment on their hind feet, they dash furiously at the hunters, butting at them, and attempting to upset horse and man. Sometimes they succeed, and then the hunter suffers terrible wounds, if not death, from the horns of the enraged animal.

Five or six bulls were killed in the attack, and the rest scattered widely over the prairie. The sight of the immense herd of cows in the distance excited the hunters, and prevented them from stopping to make any use of the bulls we had killed. We rode forward at a moderate speed for some distance, reserving the strength of our horses until we should be compelled to use their speed. At length the scouts of the herd saw us advancing, and in two or three seconds the whole herd was in motion. The first movements of the buffalo are slow, increasing in speed as they go. At the first symptoms of alarm our party raised a shout to encourage the horses, and we were suddenly flying along at full speed, the horses as much excited as their riders. The excitement was intense. At last we were close to them, and the arrows flew thick and fast into the herd. In a few moments we were in the midst of the press, firing arrows and using spears among the animals right and left.

The scene was full of wild excitement and not without danger. Some of our party were thrown from their horses and suffered severe bruises and wounds from the feet and horns of the enraged buffaloes. At last the signal of recall was given, and our party reined up to rest from the chase and dispose of the spoils.

After dismounting and hobbling the ponies, the hunters rested awhile before proceeding to the work of cutting up the buffaloes in order to take them home. When rested, the hunters began the labor of skinning and cutting up the carcasses. The animal was first placed on its knees, and its hind legs stretched out to their full length, so that the principal weight lay on the belly of the beast. The small hump of flesh about the neck was first cut out and carefully placed on one side. The skin was next divided along the back bone, and stripped down on either side. After this the animal was cut up in various pieces, all the best parts being taken and the offal left for the wolves. The fat and tallow were put in the hide, which was then slung around the necks of the packing ponies. Along each side of the pony's back was placed a pole, fastened to the animal's neck. The foot of the buffalo's hind quarter was thrust through the gambril of the forequarter, and the quarters then slung across the back of the pony and hanging down on each side. The poles keep the burden off from the sides of the pony, and prevent its back being broken. The other portions of the game were carried in a similar manner.

When the meat was brought to the camp, the women cut it into long strips, about a quarter of an inch thick. These strips were hung on sticks to dry, which operation takes several days. When thoroughly dried, the women bend it up and tie it into bundles, in which shape it is preserved for home consumption or taken to the trading posts, to be bartered for ammunition or other articles wanted by the Indians. Some parts of the buffalo, not fitted for making the dried meat, were dried by a very fierce fire until it became brittle. A buffalo hide was then spread out, with the skin uppermost, and the dried pieces of meat spread on it, and thrashed into small bits by sticks. The tallow of the buffalo was cut up, melted and poured on the powdered meat, which was then worked up until it became well mixed. Whilst still warm, it was pressed into bags made of buffalo skin, which were then sown up. When cold the mixture, known to the whites as pemican, becomes as hard as a rock, and makes good eating. The marrow bones were boiled in water for their oil, which, when extracted, was poured into the bladder of the animal. One bladder will hold eleven or twelve pounds of oil.

Buffalo are frequently killed in winter without any of the dangers experienced in the fall hunt. The alternate thawing and freezing forms a thick crust on the surface of the soft snow. The heavy animals break through this thin crust, and plunge cumbrously into the deep snow, whilst the Indian hunter glides easily on his snow shoes close to the side of the unwieldly monster, and dispatches it at his ease.

Elk, reindeer, grizzly bears, wolves, with some other animals, are killed with rifles, or arrows, frequently with the aid of dogs. The dogs are of a strong, powerful breed and are trained to catch by the ears or jaw, so that the fur is not injured. The elk and reindeer are very difficult to approach, having a keen scent, and show fight if close pressed. The attack on a grizzly bear is also dangerous, and the hunter frequently has to fight desperately for his life.

Black bears and wolves are frequently caught by a peculiar trap. A young sapling tree is bent down so that its top is but a few feet from the earth. A rope, formed of pieces of raw hide firmly twisted together, is fastened to the top of the tree and a strong double hook of iron or steel is attached to the other end of the rope. One arm of the hook is lightly caught in a log or a stake driven in the ground, and on the other arm a piece of meat is firmly attached. The bear or wolf seizes the meat, and in its endeavors to carry it off or tear it to pieces, releases the hook from the log. The tree top suddenly flies up, the hook catching the animal in the mouth or lip, and lifting it partially or completely from the ground. In this position it is found and dispatched by the hunter, when he comes to examine his traps.

Beavers are trapped in great numbers, as are martins and other fur-bearing animals. In the depth of winter the muskrat houses are sought out and pierced with strong and sharp spears which transfix the muskrats and bring them out on the points.

The skins of the animals killed are dried and cured by the women. When the hide is taken off and brought home, the women scrape off the flesh with a bone, sharpened at one end. When the skin is thoroughly scraped, small holes are cut all around it, and strings run through it, which are then lashed to the poles of the lodge inside. The fire burning in the lodge dries the skin in one night, and in the morning it is taken down and folded so as to be packed. In dressing the skins, the grease is taken off and the skins dipped in water containing the brains of a deer, after which they are boiled and stretched on four square poles tied and pushed into the ground. The skin is then scraped with a bone and kept before a slow fire until perfectly dry. It is then dipped in the brain water and scraped dry again, after which it is dipped in the water a third time, and every time the water wrung out before the skin is stretched. If it remains hairy or stiff after all this working, it is drawn over a cord as thick as a man's finger, as hard as the women can pull, and this softens it greatly. The skin is next smoked. A hole is dug in the ground, about a foot deep, in which is put a little water and some rotten wood. The skin is then sewed in a bag and hung over the smoke for about ten minutes, when it is ready for use.

The streams are well stocked with fish and these are caught in various ways. Sometimes they are speared, and some are shot with arrows and some caught by stakes arranged across the bed of the stream. When the rivers and small lakes are frozen over in winter a hole is cut in the ice and over it a little tent is made with three sticks and a blanket, so as to close out the light. The Indian lies with his face over the hole. He can then see to some depth and when a fish passes it is pierced with a short spear and brought to the surface.

There are various other ways of hunting, trapping and fishing but these will serve as specimens.

FIGHT WITH BLACKFEET

In 1861 the winter in the north was exceedingly severe and the game was compelled to seek a more southern latitude to get something to eat. We followed them down but were in great danger of perishing of famine. In this strait our only hope was in obtaining some additional supplies from the trading posts. A large detachment was therefore sent off to the post of the Hudson Bay Company for the purpose of obtaining supplies. With this band I traveled.

We arrived at the post after a long journey and were received with kindness. The few furs and skins we were able to gather up we traded for provisions but we were still in great want. That night we camped near the trading post and waited to plead our cause with the agent next day.

In the morning whilst the chief of our party and some of the leading warriors were talking to the agent and explaining to him the deplorable condition of the tribe one of the traders came into our camp. Whilst looking around and talking he came close to me and something seemed to attract his attention. Looking me in the eyes he suddenly spoke in French. I did not understand him but he immediately addressed me in Indian language, saying: "You are no Indian." I replied that I was for I never remembered anything of a life different from the one I was leading. He insisted that I was no Indian but a pale face and demanded that I should come before the agent. I was about to do so, when some of the tribe interfered to prevent me. An angry discussion now took place between the trader and the Indians, ending in my being taken before the agent himself.

On my entering the circle where the chiefs and principal warriors were conferring with the agent I was brought before the latter by the trader, and my white birth stated by him. The agent examined my features closely and endeavored to get from me by conversation whether I was a white or not. I was surprised by these statements but replied that I always considered myself an Indian. The members of the tribe present in the council were greatly disturbed when I was brought before the agent and on being appealed to strongly asserted my Indian parentage. I could not fail to remark their alarm lest I should be claimed as a white, and pondered over it for some time.

The agent was quieted for a time but was not satisfied and all the post continued to watch our movements narrowly. Next day whilst getting some provisions from the post, our chief was again asked about me and was told that no more provisions would be given the party unless I was surrendered to the whites. At this the chief returned to the camp in dismay and a brief council was held from which I was excluded. The result was that our camp was suddenly broken up and the trail immediately struck for the main body of the tribe leaving the rest of the needed supplies behind us.

On our homeward march we fell in with a party of Blackfeet who wished to rob us of our ponies and provisions. After a short skirmish the enemy was driven back, but continued to hover on our trail in order to find out our destination.

A busy scene presented itself at the camp on our arrival. Our hunters in their excursions in pursuit of game had come on traces of the Blackfeet Indians, and had followed the trail until they discovered the camp of a large war party which had evidently come out with the intention of meeting and driving us back to the north again. A grand council of the tribe was gathered and the warriors were giving their opinions as to the proper course to be pursued. Two alternatives presented themselves. One was to go back to the snows and starvation of the northern winter, and the other to meet the opposing Blackfeet and endeavor to force our way through them to the hunting grounds farther south. There was a general disposition to take the latter course, and several chiefs made stirring appeals to the pride and vengeance of the warriors. The numerous battles with the Blackfeet in former years were referred to, and the blood of the slain invoked to stir up the hearts of the warriors to revenge. Finally one of the chiefs sprang to his feet and commenced chanting an account of his warlike deeds, and boasted of what he would do in the approaching fight. Whilst he sang he danced around in a circle, stamping fiercely on the ground at every step. Every now and then he stopped to raise his war-cry.

In a few minutes another warrior sprang up and joined * the dance and song, to the music of a small drum and rattle. Then another and another leaped up, until all the fighting men of the tribe signified their intention of attacking the enemy. During the dance the utmost excitement existed, and the piercing yells worked the warriors up to mad frenzy. Knives and tomahawks were waved in the air, and all the movements of fighting and scalping an enemy gone through with.

Next day a large war party set out in the direction of the Blackfeet camp. I accompanied the party. In a short time we struck the trail of one of their bands, and followed it up till evening, when we discovered ourselves in the * vicinity of the enemy's camp. A hurried council was held, and it was decided to conceal ourselves in the woods until morning, and make the attack at sunrise. After placing sentinels to keep watch of the camp, our party lay down among the brush and waited for day.

At the first dawn of day we were all awake and creeping stealthily towards the edge of the wood, beyond which the camp was pitched. As we neared the opening the Blackfeet discovered our approach and raised an alarm. In an instant there was great confusion in the camp, and their warriors were rushing backwards and forwards, snatching up their weapons and attempting to seek a^ place of shelter from the coming attack.

At this moment our war chief blew a blast on a horn carried by him, and at the signal a volley of shot and arrows was fired into the camp. Several of the Blackfeet were killed and wounded, and the others ran to the woods for protection. Some of our warriors dashed into the opening, cut down the wounded and rapidly scalped them, raising a terrible war whoop as each bloody scalp was hatched from the head of the prostrate foe. As soon as 'he work was done they again sought the protection of the trees.

The fight was now conducted from behind the trees and every one fought after his own fashion. Sometimes one side appeared to gain the advantage, and then the fortune would change. Hours passed away, and both parties were very much scattered, but the Blackfeet were generally in retreat. At last they broke up and fled, when our warriors returned, plundered the camp of what little was left in it, and took the trail homewards. A number of scalps were borne home in triumph.

Three captives were taken and their arms tied firmly to their sides, after which they were driven before us to the camp. On arriving there the party was received with shouts of triumph, and the women and children made a tremendous noise. Some of the squaws who had lost husbands in battle came up to the captives and loaded them with insults and abuse, shaking their fists in the face of the victims and acting like mad women. The captives remained perfectly indifferent to these insults, and" made no sign of being aware that the women were in existence.

When the party entered the camp, the prisoners were tied to different posts. The warriors then indulged in a great rejoicing. "Snakyeye" or whisky was brought out and drank. The warriors boasted of their deeds in battle and divided the captives. Then they sprang up in a wild dance, and menaced the captives with their knives and tomahawks. One of the Blackfeet replied in contemptuous words to the taunts of the Copper-Heads, which so exasperated them that several of the latter at once rushed to the posts and tomahawked two of the captives. The third was saved by a chief of our tribe, who proposed that he should be burned instead of tomahawked.

This proposal met with favor, and preparations were at once made for carrying it into execution. Wood was brought and piled up around the victim until it ascended above his knees. He was then tormented by descriptions of the horrible sufferings that he was to endure, but the threats failed to shake his constancy in the least.

As soon as all the preparations were complete, a large number of warriors and squaws encircled the victim and commenced a wild dance. Fire was applied to the pile, and in a few moments the flames ascended around the body of the captive Blackfoot. He commenced chanting a death-song, and did not stop till life was extinct. The dance was kept up around the stake until the body was consumed, when a yell was given and the assemblage dispersed to their lodges.

Next day another council was held, and it was decided not to go any farther to the south, but to return and get through the winter as well as possible in a territory where we should be out of the Blackfeet range. Accordingly our tents were struck and packed, the ponies loaded, and we once more took the northward trail.

MARRIAGE

The fact that the traders at the Hudson Bay Company's post had claimed me to be of white birth was communicated to the principal chief after the war excitement of the latter was over, and caused considerable anxiety on his part. Nothing was said to me about it but I could see that the old chief feared my escape and that the tribe would be made to suffer some punishment at the hands of the-whites for my captivity. I had always considered myself as an Indian captured from some other tribe and could not yet think it possible that I was one of the pale faces. With the return of Summer the tribe again sought the Northern regions and I had almost forgotten the affair at the trading post. The old chief, Owash-kah-ke-naw, appeared to have taken a great liking to me and in September of that year (1851) he gave me his youngest daughter, Tefronia (Tame Deer) to be my squaw. She was then nineteen and a handsome Indian woman. My own name in Copper-Head language is Owah-owah-kish-me-wah. By this squaw I have two children, Tefronia, a girl now over five years of age, and Tululee, a boy over two years old.

After marrying his daughter I was kept by the old chief around the village and was not allowed to join any expeditions in the lower country. Three years passed in this manner and my girl was born. The tribe once more moved farther south and the old chief become anxious about my being claimed by the whites. One day he told me that if I went south with the tribe I must be tattooed, so that I could be identified by them in case I should be carried off by the traders under pretence that I was of white parentage. I did not consent to this but was then told that there was no choice left me as it was the will of the chief that it should be done.

Next day I was seized by two men of the tribe and made to lie on my back along a log. I was next bound down so that I could neither move my head, body, hands or feet. My breast was bared and one of the Indians came forward to do the work of tattooing.

First he took a sharp knife and made some light incisions down my breast so that small strips of skin were cut. These he peeled off and threw on one side. My agony was intense but I did not wish to be considered a coward so I held my tongue, though the pain made me bite my lips till the blood came; other similar strips were next taken off at the distance of about an inch, but parallel with the first marks. I now suffered tortures and was racked with an intense thirst. The attendant Indians brought me water and poured it into my mouth and over my head to , keep me from fainting.

Parallel strips were now cut at right angles to the first incisions and then other strips at right angles to the second series of cuts. Some other incisions were also made but by this time I was almost insensible to pain. During these operations a smooth stone had been remaining in a strong fire and as the marks were all cut the stone was taken up and applied to my lacerated breast. The pain for the moment was maddening but the effect was to sear the wounds and stop the bleeding. I was now released from my fastenings and sought my lodge, with marks on breast that I still carry and shall to my dying day.

After this time I was allowed to go with the rest of the tribe in the excursions to the southern part of the territory over which we ranged. About two years since I joined the half yearly train that left for the Selkirk settlement on the Red River and for St. Paul's.

As I stated before, the train starts twice a year—in the Spring and Fall, laden with furs and brings back supplies of various kinds. The journey occupies about six "moons" each way and one "moon" is allowed for stoppage at St. Paul's, so that the trains meet about half way on the journey. A large number of Indians travel in these trains so as to fight their way down in case of resistance by hostile Indians.

Previous to starting on the journey all the furs, skins and other articles intended to be taken down together with dried meats for the journey, were packed in readiness to be carried by ponies and elks, or by the squaws in the manner already described. When everything was ready a grand Council was held, at which the old men of the tribe sat around the council fire, smoking their pipes in silence. Then the principal chief arose and appointed one of the subordinate chiefs to the command of the party, giving him in a few words some general instructions relative to the policy to be adopted in dealing with the whites and exhorting the warriors attached to the party to

33

drive from the face of the earth all who should oppose their progress. Particular charge was given that I should be kept away from the whites as much as possible, and watch kept that I might not be stolen from them by the pale faces.

The old chief sat down, and the newly appointed chief of the expedition rose and made a speech, as did some others of the tribe. Then there were some dances, after which the Council broke up and all retired to their lodges.

Early next morning the party set out on their journey. The ponies and elks were loaded with packs, the squaws carried some articles attached to the straps passed across their forehead, and the men rode or walked in single file. The journey was long and tedious, day after day passing with but few incidents to change the monotony of our progress. Hunting parties started off occasionally in pursuit of game for the support of the band, and met at appointed places, but the main body kept advancing steadily in the one direction.

Only four hours was allowed for sleep, when fires were lit and we all lay around in our blankets, with our feet to the fire, and heads outward. There are two reasons for adopting this mode of sleeping: it keeps the feet warm, which is very important, and it allows more people to sleep around one fire than would be possible in any other. position. On stopping for sleep the ponies were hobbled in such a manner that they could feed or sleep, but could not run away. Sentinels were posted to prevent the camp being surprised either by wild animals or by hostile Indians.

As soon as the time was up the signal was given and the whole camp was speedily awake and ready for resuming the journey. A hasty meal was despatched, and then, after determining the course to be taken, the band set forward. There were no fixed hours for meals, and no stoppage for that purpose, but each person took a piece of dried meat whenever he became hungry, and gnawed away as he felt disposed.

The country through which we passed changed from dense forests to barren plains, and then again to rolling prairies, high hills, and grassy valleys. When large streams opposed our progress there was a halt on the banks, and preparations were made for swimming across. The packs were disposed of so as not to be wetted and then each animal, led by an Indian, was brought to the stream and swam across to the other side. When the animals and their burdens had all safely been got over, the remaining men and squaws plunged in and swam over. The very young children were carried on the backs of the swimmers or floated across on boards, which the mothers pushed before them.

At the North Pass of the Rocky Mountains the band crossed from the west to the east side. The crossing was the work of time and difficulty, both animals and Indians having to creep slowly up the rugged heights of the Pass. Sometimes we were many hours making half a mile progress,-and great caution was requisite to prevent serious accidents among the precipices around which we crept. At times we wound our way through a deep gorge, on either side of which the enormous walls of rock towered far overhead. Then a toilsome ascent brought us on an elevation from which we looked down on rugged peaks and deep clefts below. At length the difficulties and dangers of the pass were over, and we emerged on the rolling land to the east of the mountains.

Up to this time we had met with no hostile Indians, or, at least, none that attempted to molest us. We were now in the territory hunted by the Bloods and Blackfeet, and were therefore not without fears of an attack. On the second day after leaving the Pass I joined a hunting party and set out in pursuit of buffalo. The party consisted of thirty hunters, all well-armed either for the chase or war. A herd of bulls was discovered at a distance, and we rode quietly towards them.

As we rose on a ridge that commanded a wide view of the country, we became aware of a party of mounted Indians at no great distance from us, in pursuit of the same herd of buffalo. They appeared to have discovered us at the same time, and both parties drew up to reconnoitre. In numbers both were nearly equal, and there appeared to be little doubt that the opposing band were some of our old enemies, the Blackfeet. A short council was held without dismounting, and there was a question as to the policy of fighting them on the spot, or of falling back on the main body and keeping prepared for the larger band of Blackfeet that probably lay in our course towards the Selkirk settlement.

The question was settled, without farther discussion on our part, by the appearance of the Blackfeet galloping towards us. Our party dashed forward to meet them, and as the two bands neared each other, rapid discharges of bullets and arrows were made by both sides. I received a rifle ball in my instep, and was thrown from my pony by a Blackfoot that dashed against me.

The fight was desperate, and several scalps were taken on both sides. A Blackfoot warrior singled me out for combat, and for some time we fought hand to hand. Severe blows were given on both sides, and I felt faint from loss of blood, having received a frightful gash in the thigh from a tomahawk, besides an ugly knife wound in one knee and in the calf of one leg. In the end the hostile party was repulsed, though with severe loss on our side, and we retreated to the main body of our party.

Here my wounds were found to be of sufficient importance to require some attention. I was lashed to a log in order to prevent my writhing during the process of dressing the wounds. The gashes were then cleaned out and washed with water. Some kinnikenick bark was chewed up and a mixed with tobacco, which was then put into the wound to stop the bleeding. The washing and dressing was repeated until the bleeding had completely stopped. One of the men took a thin buckskin thong and sewed up the wounds by piercing the skin and running the thong through it. Only two stitches were made for each gash. The pain of this operation was intense, and was more difficult to bear than the original wounds. The marks of the stitches are still visible on my person.

Whether the defeat of the smaller party of Blackfeet had discouraged the larger band, or whether there was no large party in the neighborhood at that time, I cannot tell, but it was certain that we were not again troubled with them during our journey. Occasionally a straggling hunter* or two would be seen, but they always made off before any of our warriors could reach them.

We had now reached the hunting grounds of the Selkirkers, or colonists of English, Scotch, French and half-breeds, who lived on the territory granted to Lord Selkirk for the purpose of establishing a colony there. The land from the Rocky Mountains to the Red River is pleasant to look at, and rich with game of all kinds. Buffalo, deer, and smaller game, range in great numbers over the plains, and the hunters and trappers of the Selkirk colony are scattered in the season, in all directions over this splendid territory. Soon after getting into this country we fell in with some trappers who were returning to the settlements, and they traveled with our train as far as we went in their direction.

In the course of our journey with them, they noticed my appearance and spoke to me of my resemblance to whites, even though disguised with paint as I was. They became interested in me and taught me several words of English, which I learned very rapidly.

On reaching the Selkirk settlements we camped for a few days in order to rest awhile before striking the Red River trail, and to do a little trading with the settlers. Here the traders who had been teaching me English told some of the other whites about me, and I was visited by several Selkirkers. After conversing with me for some time they summoned the chief, and charged the tribe with having stolen me when a child from the whites. He denied it, but the Selkirkers became more determined in their suspicions, and demanded that I should be given up to them, threatening to take me by force if not surrendered peaceably. I was appealed to as to what my wishes were on this subject. So much had been told me by the traders about my having probably been stolen from my white parents, that I had become anxious to know something about the facts, and I frankly said so. On this the Selkirkers became more eager to have me left with them, but our chief dissuaded me from consenting, by representing that I had no clue to my parents, even if it was true that I had been stolen from the whites, but that if I returned to the tribe, I could undoubtedly get part of my history from the old chief, who would also probably give me leave to go, in case I chose to hunt up my family. With this I was content, and the

Selkirkers let me go after exacting a solemn promise from the chief and principal warriors that I should be allowed to proceed in search of my parents if I felt disposed to do so.

With the dawn of day we again set forward on our journey, taking the Red River trail towards St. Paul. The trip between the Selkirk settlements and St. Paul occupies from thirty to forty days, and passes through the battle ground of the Siouxs and Chippewas. Several times we came on small parties of the Siouxs, but had no more than short skirmishes with them, our numbers being too formidable for them to attack us. About two days journey from the Selkirk settlements we came to the settlement of Osha-wkapee, inhabited by French and half breeds. From this point we passed over a magnificent rolling country interspersed with occasional woods and watered by several streams.

Whilst crossing this country we met the Red River settlement train returning from their trading journey to St. Paul. The train was composed of four or five hundred ox carts in single file, with drivers on foot, or riding on the wagons, hunters and guards mounted on ponies, and women and children riding with camp fixtures in covered wagons.

The Selkirkers' wagons are of a peculiar kind, no iron being used in any part of their construction. There is but one pair of wheels, having felloes about six inches thick. There about fourteen spokes to a wheel, and these spokes are about three feet long. The linch pins, axles, and in fact everything about the carts, are of wood, very massive and cumbrous. No grease is used on the axles, so that an incessant groaning and creaking is kept up. The body of the cart is nothing but a frame work similar to the wood-racks used in the lower country. Sometimes a tilt covering is used for the wagons that carry the women and children. Each cart is drawn by one ox fastened to the shafts by straps of raw hide. One man has charge of five wagons, a strap passing from the tail of one wagon over the horns of the ox drawing the wagon immediately following it. When the driver whips the first ox it starts forward, and the oxen in the squad of carts attached to the moving wagon have to start at the same time.

The drivers of these trains are mixed French Canadians, English, Scotch, and half 'breeds. In most cases the women are Indians, and these travel with the train to do the cooking and general work of the camp. When they camp for the night they bring all the wagons into a close circle with the shafts outwards. Immediately inside of this circle each ox is tied to the cart to which it belongs, and within this inner circle of cattle the ponies are picketed. The tents are then pitched within the whole, sentinels placed, and the camp composed to sleep.

Salutations were exchanged with the Selkirkers' train as we passed, and our journey was again resumed. At length we arrived at our village a short distance from St. Anthony, and here preparations were made for staying one month, during which the trading was to be done.

In this time our furs and skins were taken down to St, Paul, and, by means of our interpreter were traded for whiskey, powder, rifles, provisions of various kinds, weapons, and such other articles as were needed by us. During these tradings I practiced myself in speaking English, and could soon talk so as to make myself understood. I had some conversations with the settlers, and became more anxious to discover the facts in relation to my supposed parentage. I determined that as soon as I went back I would demand my history from the old chief, and if I could obtain any trace from him, I would then prosecute the search after my parents.

When the trading was over and the supplies brought back to the camp, there was a grand feast given, and the camp became a scene of drunken debauchery for several days. Whiskey was drunk in great quantities, and many quarrels took place between the men. As they had taken the precaution of putting away their weapons before the drinking began, no one was killed in the quarrels.

At length our time was up, the Indians got over their debauch, and every thing was made ready for the return trip. We were soon on our way, and marching with our faces to the North.

The journey to our northern headquarters had no particular incident to interest me, my mind being now full of the idea that I had white relatives and friends, and that the savage life I had led for so many years was not the one for which I was born. I longed to reach our village once more, that I might question the old chief as to my history. At last we reached the main body of our tribe. I was rejoiced to meet my Tefronia and the children once more, but at the same time a new feeling had entered my breast.

I waited impatiently two or three days until the rejoicings caused by our return should have passed away, and then I sought out the venerable chief, O-wash-kah-ke-naw, now over eighty years old, and begged him to tell me truly the secret of my birth.

For some time the chief bade me go back to my lodge and be content with what I already knew, but, finding that I was resolute in discovering the facts, he told me to await a few days in patience, and then he would give his decision. I returned to my lodge in much agitation, for it was evident that the chief knew something that had hitherto been concealed from me. I had been so long accustomed to savage - life that I remembered no other.

A council of the leading chiefs only, called on the following day, which I rightly considered was to consult on the course to be pursued in respect to my demand. At last I was summoned before the great chief and a few leading warriors, and was instructed as to the course allotted for me.

I was then informed that when a child I had been stolen from the whites by a band of Canadian Indians who had by this course revenged themselves on the whites for some real or fancied wrongs; that I had passed through the hands of several tribes and had at last, as I already knew, been sold by the Siouxs to the Snakes, and remained with them until their union with the Copper Heads. The decision of the head men of the tribe was that I should join the train about to set out for the settlements, and should then proceed in company with a few picked warriors, to visit the remnants of the tribes in whose possession I had once been, in order to learn more of my former history. At the same time I was sworn to return to the tribe within a year after I left the train at St. Paul, and to ensure the fulfillment of this condition, my wife and children were to be retained in the old chiefs family at the headquarters of the tribe. To

41

these conditions I freely consented, and waited eagerly for the day when I should set out on my journey.

At last the day arrived and I took a farewell of my wife and children. The thought of them checked a little my eagerness to set out, but at length I left them, fully intending to return as soon as I could discover something of my former history.

RETURN TO ST. PAUL

The snows of winter had begun to fall when our party set out on the route I had so recently traveled. The present company was placed under command of a son of the principal chief, he being also the brother of my wife. There is no reason for again describing the route, as we traveled in the same trail that we pursued with the former party, and this time there were no incidents of consequence to diversify the monotony of the progress. About the beginning of April, 1859, we reached our camping ground near St. Anthony, and on the 10th of that month I arrived with a detachment of the tribe at St. Paul. We remained here a few days, making inquiries of the Siouxs and Chippewas that occasionally came in to trade, and from them I obtained a clue to farther discoveries.

On the 16th of April I obtained leave from the chief to set out on investigations, promising faithfully to return to St. Paul in July, when the train would be ready to return.

To aid me in my researches I was accompanied part of the way by the chief himself and some members of the tribe, and our party was furnished with three ponies and five dogs. In pursuance to the information obtained from the Sioux and Chippewas, we proceeded in search of a party of Winnebagoes said to' be located in Northern Wisconsin. After traveling some days we reached the Wisconsin river, and following it towards its source came on the Winnebagoes, who were making sugar in the woods. From them I obtained the particulars of my purchase by them from the Paw Paws, and was directed to a family yet living in Michigan who could probably give me some farther information.

Filled with hope I started, in company with my brother-in-law and the other Indians, for Chicago. We traveled through the woods and across the country, I acting as interpreter, being now able to speak English with tolerable proficiency. Before reaching that city I was taken sick, and on arriving there I fell into the hands of some sympathizing persons who placed me under medical care. My escort, finding that I had become so sick that I could neither prosecute my researches for some time nor return with them, quitted me and returned to St. Paul, leaving me only my faithful dog, Nawah.

I was very sick and do not remember much for two or three weeks, when I found myself in a hospital, with my long hair cut off close to my head and the paint scrubbed from my skin. To get it off they had used hot water, soap and sand, and in the process had transformed me from an Indian to a white man. I remained in the hospital for more than five weeks, and then I was discharged as cured, though still very weak.

On letting me go they gave me a suit of white men's clothing instead of my Indian costume, leaving me nothing but my stone pipe and my scalping knife. Nawah and I at once set out on our adventures, and my steps were directed towards the place where the Paw Paw family was said to reside. I found them after walking for two days, and then was directed to a small village of Pottawottomies in Branch county, Michigan. I walked to the place described, sleeping in the woods at night as had been customary with me, but I soon found that I could no longer do so with safety. With my long hair cut off and without my blanket and furs, I was unprepared for camping out. The result was that I caught a severe inflammation in my eyes that increased to an extent threatening my sight. I could no longer bear the light and had to walk with my head down.

On reaching the Pottawottomies I found they consisted of four families and their chief, Mr. Macgwagor. They had settled down to civilized life and were living as farmers. Mr. Macgwagor remembered the whole transaction in relation to my purchase from the Canadian Indians, he having been present at the transfer. He said the Canadian Indians had stated at the time that they had taken me from the south side of Lake Erie, and that," from their description, the party had probably brought me from Ohio, as they spoke of having crossed the Sandusky river during the journey on which they fell in with me.

On learning this I set out for Detroit and crossed over into Canada, but without obtaining much farther information among the few semi-civilized Indians and half-breeds that I met with there. All I

44

could gather was that I had probably been taken from somewhere in the vicinity of Cleveland.

I now retraced my steps to Detroit and proceeded into Ohio, telling my story as I went and requesting information. At Fremont I fell in with a man who listened to my story with attention and remarked that he had formerly heard of a family named Todd, who had lost a little boy from the neighborhood of Cleveland a number of years ago. Acting under his suggestions, on the following day I got on the railroad train and came to Cleveland, where I arrived in the latter part of August.

I was in Cleveland about one day, making inquiries relative to the Todd family and telling my story, but without getting any information that was of use. The Todd family had removed many years since, and I could not learn their whereabouts. I had begun to despair of ever finding traces of my parents when a friendly colored man who had met me and learned my story, took me to the office of the *Cleveland Daily Herald* for the purpose of telling my story to the editors. We succeeded in finding one of them, Mr. J. H. A. Bone, in the office, together with another gentleman. I told my story to them and was cross-questioned by them very closely. In the end I was directed to an old citizen of the place for the purpose of making inquiries, and was told to call again and tell the result.

The person to whom I was directed was out of town, and I learned nothing farther that night. Several persons took considerable interest in my story and wished me well in my journeyings. Next morning I was on the street when I saw some furs and other articles of Esquimaux dress at the door of a building, and was told that a panorama of the Arctic regions was on exhibition, and that one of the men belonging to it—Thomas Hickey—had been in the far North. I went up to see him, and to him and the proprietor, Mr. La Rue, told my story.

I then accompanied Mr. La Rue to the office of the *Herald*, and there I again met Mr. Bone, who made me repeat my story and then printed it with a request that any person possessing information of probable use to the "Indian Captive" would at once furnish it.

The interest taken in my story by the editors of the *Cleveland Herald* has been the means of my return to my relatives.

I remained in Cleveland several days and my story excited much interest. Some persons furnished me with portions of clothing of which I stood in need, and I was furnished with food and sleeping room at one of the hotels. The people at the house were surprised at my refusal to sleep in a bed and to eat cooked meat or anything that had salt in it, but I could not endure the method of eating or sleeping used by civilized white people.

In a few days I learned that some persons in Warren, O., could probably give me some information, and thither I went, the Cleveland and Mahoning Railroad Company taking me without my paying fare. On arriving there I found that the people to whom I was directed had gone out of town to attend a camp meeting in Mahoning county. Some persons going to the meeting invited me to accompany them, and in their company I arrived at the camp meeting.

A short time sufficed to convince me that I had got on the wrong track and that I was not the missing son of Joseph Todd. Great interest was, however, occasioned by my story, and many questions were put to me. I showed the Presiding Elder papers given me in proof of my belonging to the Indian tribe and related my adventures. Finally I showed them my dog, scalping knife and pipe. The Presiding Elder, Mr. Anson Brazee, was so much interested in my story that he got me to repeat it to the whole meeting. I remained with these people throughout the meeting, and before it broke up I became thoroughly convinced of the truth of the Christian religion and joined the church of the United Brethren. In token that I had forever abandoned the bloody practices of heathenism I broke my scalping knife in two, giving the handle and part of the blade to Elder Brazee, and the other part of the blade to a circuit preacher, the Rev. William McIntyre. When the camp broke up I accompanied the elder and some of the ministers to a conference in Stark county, and from thence went to Williamsfield, Ashtabula county, where I stayed with some farmers belonging to the church of the United Brethren.

After staying with these good people about a fortnight I went to Monroe, Ashtabula county, in search of some information that I expected to get there, but failed to obtain anything of use. I then accepted the invitation of Elder Brazee and went to his house in Pierpont, Ashtabula county, where I stayed a short time. From there I went to Conneautville, thence to Clark's Corners and to Connorsville. From that place the minister sent a letter to Cleveland stating that I had gone into Pennsylvania, and giving directions where I probably could be heard of.

I continued to wander from place to place, wherever the faintest hope existed of my getting any information, and in this way I visited Erie, Waterford, Wattsburgh, and finally reached Warren, Pa., where the Rev. William McIntyre was stationed. I remained with him a short time ana then retraced my steps to Ashtabula county, after which I again returned to Mr. McIntyre's and from thence went to Columbus, Pa.

My hopes of finding my relatives had now almost died out. Nearly six months had passed, but I seemed no nearer the object of my search than I was when I left St. Paul. Wearied out with fruitless efforts, I had resolved to make one more attempt, and if that failed, to abandon the search for ever and return to my tribe on the approach of spring. My eyes remained very bad, and I therefore labored under great disadvantages, having to be careful lest the inflammation should increase and destroy my sight. I had gone to school for a few days in Pennsylvania, but the state of my eyes compelled me reluctantly to abandon the idea for the present, at least.

From Columbus I went to Sugar Grove, Warren county, Pa., close to the New York State line. My intention was to remain there a day or two, and then set out for the Cattaraugus Indian Reservation where I intended making my last effort at obtaining information. If I failed there I meant either to return to the Rev. Mr. McIntyre's residence and attend school for the winter, or go into Canada and remain with the Indians until spring, when it would be time to return to St. Paul. On the 18th or November I was at Sugar Grove when Mr. W. T. Smith, a farmer living in New York State, just across the line, drove up with his wagon early in the morning to take me to his house, where I was to stay a few days previous to leaving for the Cattaraugus Reservation. I little dreamed, when I arrived at the house, that the end of my journeyings was so near, and that the object of the search which I had almost abandoned in despair was already within a few hours of attainment.

FOUND AT LAST

The narration of the circumstances which led to the discovery of Matthew Brayton by his relatives requires us to go back a little from the point to which his account has brought the reader. The intervening years between the loss of Matthew Brayton by his relatives and the present time have caused many changes in the neighborhood once so excited in consequence of that loss. The red men clung for many years to their last foothold in Ohio. Four years after the loss of the boy, the Delawares left their village below Upper Sandusky, and set out for their new homes farther west. Two years afterwards the Senecas extinguished their council fires and sought a resting place nearer the Rocky Mountains. But the Wyandots held tenaciously to their homes, and eighteen years passed away before they finally consented to abandon Ohio to the exclusive occupation of the white race.

Fine farms now cover the site of the waste land and woods over and through which the weary hunt for the missing boy was conducted day after day. Towns and villages have sprung up where humble log cabins here and there stood in the incipient clearing, and the huts of the red skins have passed away forever.

The sturdy farmer, Elijah Brayton, who once returned to his cabin from the weary journey to Chillicothe after millstones, and was met by news that made the blood forsake his parental heart in a sudden rush, had passed by some years the allotted period of man's life, and is fast progressing towards his fourscore years. William, the boy of sixteen who had set out with his little brother on that search for stray cattle, but had returned without him, has reached the meridian of life, and sees around him a young family springing up. Long since, the paternal cabin near the Tymochte Creek has disappeared, and two or three miles away from it, somewhere in the direction where the two brothers had separated thirty-four years ago, a fine brick house has become the dwelling of the oldest son of Elijah Brayton. Up at Springville, some five or six miles farther to the northwest, and at no great distance from the trail on which the young boy was borne off by the thieving Canadian Indians, lives another brother,

Peter, and one of the married sisters. Here also lives the patriarch himself. There are other sisters who mourned when their brother was lost, and they too are married. A son and daughter born to the patriarch of the family after the loss of Matthew, have long since died, and another son, Asa, younger yet, pursues the practice of medicine in the adjoining town of Carey.

The publication of the "Indian Captive's" narrative in the *Cleveland Herald* was the means of creating considerable interest in his fortunes. The story was extensively copied, and several letters were received by the editors of that paper from people in different sections of the country who had lost children many years ago; it was supposed by means of Indians. None of these letters afforded any clue by which the Indian Captive could trace out his family.

A weekly paper containing the story, copied from the *Cleveland Herald*, was sent by a friend to the Braytons, and this first gave them an idea that there might be a possibility of recovering the missing member of the family. On the 26th of September, one month after the first publication of the narrative, Dr. Asa Brayton wrote to the editors of the *Herald*, stating the manner in which he had met with the article, and giving some particulars of the method in which his brother Matthew had been lost. About a week afterwards a cousin of the Doctor called at the office of that paper, and made inquiries respecting the Indian Captive. He was followed in a few days by Mr. Peter Brayton, one of the brothers of the missing Matthew, who went to Warren, O., in search of the "Captive," but lost trace of him there and returned discouraged.

The interest in the subject did not abate, and from time to time the Herald gave some intelligence regarding the wanderings of the "Indian Captive." The more the Braytons considered the matter the stronger was their desire to satisfy themselves, and on the tenth of November, William Brayton, the eldest brother, who had accompanied Matthew on the morning of the day when the latter was lost, set out with the determination of not returning until he could satisfy himself as to whether the "Indian Captive" was identical with his lost brother, or not.

Previous to setting out, William was charged by his father to examine the man for two marks by which his identity could probably be established. One was a scar on the top of the head, caused by a razor cut which the father had made in lancing a boil, and the other was a scar on the great toe of the right foot, resulting from the cut of an axe.

William Brayton came to Cleveland and learned that the person of whom he was in search had been heard of in Northern Pennsylvania, and was directed where to go. At the place pointed out he struck the trail of the "Captive," and traced him to Sugar Grove. Here he learned that the man had crossed the State line into New York. The chase was too near at an end to allow any delay, so Mr. Brayton took along a doctor as witness of the interview, and set out for the house of Mr. Smith, where it was said that the "Captive" had gone.

It was seven o'clock in the evening when the two arrived at the house, and the daylight was fast fading into darkness. They knocked at the door, and, in response to an invitation from within, entered the house. A man, with his boots off, was drying his feet at the fire. Mr. Brayton stepped forward eagerly and enquired where the "folks" were, and was told that they were out doing some work in the yard. Mr. Brayton said he wanted them called in, and wished a light struck at once, following up the request with the question whether the man to whom he spoke was the "Indian Captive." On being told in the affirmative he became greatly agitated and proceeded at once to get a light, The "Captive" hastily drew on his boots, buckled his dog to his belt, and drew back with suspicion from the strangers. As soon as the light was obtained Mr. Brayton bade the "Captive" bare his head, and then both he and his companion examined the spot where his father had told them to search for the scar. The emotion of William Brayton may be imagined when the scar was plainly revealed to his eyes, unmistakable in its character, and situated precisely where he had been told to look for it. In an agitated voice he bade the man take the boot from his right foot, which was done, and there too, was a scar visible, just where it had been described to exist.

The emotions of William Brayton may be imagined, but cannot be portrayed. The brother for whose loss he had always reproached himself was at length found through his means, and the sorrows of thirty-four years were at an end. For some minutes he paced up and down the room, his whole frame convulsed with agitation. Then he turned to the cause of all this emotion, who sat perfectly astonished at the proceedings, and the "Indian Captive" was declared to be the long lost Matthew Brayton.

A letter was at once sent home, containing the glad news of the discovery, and, as soon as possible, the reunited brothers set out in the same direction.

At every station on the road home, crowds gathered, and at Carey, where they were expected to stop, hundreds were collected—old men who had searched for the lost boy—aged mothers who had held him in their arms—young men who had heard the story narrated by their parents. But the couple stopped five miles north of Carey, at Adrian Station, and at once started for William Brayton's house.

Here the family were gathered. The old man, seventy-three years of age, but still hale and vigorous—the brothers and sisters. When the eldest brother entered with his charge the intense feeling that prevailed the hearts of all in the room can scarcely be imagined—cannot be described. The aged father arose, placed his trembling hand on the head of the stranger, and searched for the scar, which he could scarcely distinguish through the mist that filled his eyes. Then he knelt to examine the foot. For a moment every breath was hushed, and the hearts of the other relatives almost ceased to beat. Then the old man tottered to his feet, and with a gush of tears—the stream of affection that had been pent up for the third of a century— fell on the neck of his son—Matthew Brayton! It is useless to attempt a description of the scene that followed. The father that had so long secretly mourned for his child, the household pet; the brother who never forgot that it was from his company that the little boy had passed away to a mysterious fate; the other brother who had been his playmate; the sisters who had fondled their little brother in infancy—all were gathered to share in that happy meeting. There was one absent whose presence was needed to make the cup of joy full to overflowing, but her motherly heart might perhaps even then be rejoicing in Heaven for the happiness on earth.

The news of the return spread like wildfire. The return was on Thursday the 17th of November. For days afterwards the house was besieged by anxious people eager to see the "boy" so long lost, and so strangely found. Old men who had shared with zeal in that weary and hopeless search thirty-four years ago, came up, and all who had known him as a little boy, acknowledged the identity.

At present Matthew Brayton, the hero of these strange adventures, is residing with his father and brothers, and has become somewhat reconciled to civilized life. He has abandoned his design of returning to the Indians, and is endeavoring to fit himself for the different lot now assigned him. He has attended school as frequently as the state of his eyes permitted, and can now read a little, as well as converse very readily in the English language. After his thirty-four years of wanderings and hardships it is to be hoped that he will now be content to remain among his family and partake to the full of the blessings of civilization.

****

The foregoing is a reproduction of a book published in 1860, giving the strange history of this Indian Captive. After returning to civilization, he resided for a few months in Carey and Fostoria, and made several lecture tours giving an account of his adventures and the manners and customs of the Indians.

This mode of life was too much of a change from the wild life he had been living, and when the war of the Rebellion [American Civil War] broke out he enlisted in an Indiana Regiment, and went to the South to fight for his country. He proved a brave soldier, but while in the service he was taken dangerously ill, and after a short sickness died at Pittsburgh Landing in 1862.

BIG BYTE BOOKS is your source for great lost history!

Made in the USA
Coppell, TX
18 April 2020

20875458R00035